crafting
with kids

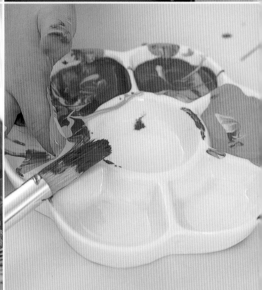

photography by
vanessa davies

catherine woram

crafting

with kids

**creative fun for
children aged 3–10**

RYLAND
PETERS
& SMALL
LONDON NEW YORK

First published in the United
Kingdom in 2006 by
Ryland Peters & Small
20–21 Jockey's Fields
London WC1R 4BW
www.rylandpeters.com

10 9 8 7 6 5 4 3 2

ISBN-10: 1-84597-251-1
ISBN-13: 978-1-84597-251-6

A CIP record for this book is
available from the British Library.

Printed and bound in China

Senior designer Catherine Griffin
Commissioning editor Annabel
Morgan
Picture research Emily Westlake
Production Gordana Simakovic
Art director Anne-Marie Bulat
Publishing director Alison Starling

Text and styling Catherine Woram

contents

get creative and crafty...

I must confess to a lifelong passion for crafts – my mother remembers finding me on her sewing machine at the age of seven, inserting a zip into a skirt I had just made. She didn't know whether to be cross that I had used the machine without her permission or delighted at her eldest daughter's budding sewing skills! She still has many of the items we crafted as children, and it is this aspect of crafting that makes it so appealing. There is nothing better than a handmade gift or card from a child, because it is unique.

The projects in this book cover a wide selection of different crafting techniques, from papier mâché to tie-dye. Each project is accompanied by step-by-step photographs, and there are suggestions for other items that can be made using the same basic technique. If your kids love crafting (and most do), it's a good idea to create a craft box or to devote a kitchen cupboard to craft materials. Squirrel away lengths of string and ribbon, scraps of fabric and left-over wrapping paper. Many of the projects make use of basic household items such as newspapers and jam jars, which is a great way of recycling them. Teach your child to look after their tools, and to clean them after they have finished crafting.

One of the most rewarding aspects of the creation of the book was seeing how the children enjoyed the crafts. My daughters, Jessica (aged eight) and Anna (aged six), helped with many projects and were a constant source of inspiration. I'm sure that you'll enjoy making the projects in the book as much as your children will, and that your friends and relatives will delight in receiving them as gifts too.

paint

Any painting undertaken in our house inevitably ends up with the children painting parts of themselves too! So, if a project requires them to paint themselves, they are sure to enjoy it. Paint-and-bake ceramic kits that can be 'fired' in a domestic oven are ideal for this project.

finger- and hand-painting

YOU WILL NEED:
plate or other object to be decorated • specialist paint for china • paintbrushes in various sizes • saucers to hold the paint

paint hands In separate saucers or on a paint tray, put out a small amount of each of the paint colours to be used. Use a thick brush to apply the paint to the palm of the hand. Make sure that the paint is not too thick. It's a good idea to keep a damp cloth close by in case of accidents.

practise printing Before attempting to decorate your plate, or other chosen object, help your child to practise first, to get the technique right. The hand needs to be pressed as flat as possible, with the fingers slightly splayed to show the shape. Once the printing technique has been mastered on paper, you can move on to the real thing.

print on plate Clean off any excess paint from the practise run, and reapply fresh paint to the hand. You can use one colour, or you can paint different fingers in different colours. Press the hand flat with fingers splayed, as before. Carefully lift the hand off the plate and allow the paint to dry.

finish off Apply a coat of paint to the fingertips and print around the edge of the plate to create a border. The child may also like to write his or her name on the plate. To fix the paint, bake the item in the oven, following the manufacturer's instructions, or take it to a pottery café to be fired.

framed picture

Fingertips can be used to create all manner of shapes or designs, including animals, flowers and abstract patterns. This pretty bouquet of flowers in a palette of bright pinks, oranges and reds was made using the fingertips. The simple vase was painted in using a brush. Fingertip prints were also used to decorate the painted frame.

painted plates

A palm print decorates the centre of this plate, while the border is finger-painted in alternate colours of red and mauve. To celebrate the birth of a new baby, try painting the soles of the baby's feet and decorating a plate, to keep as a memory of those tiny feet.

painted tray

A simple wooden tray decorated by your child makes a delightful gift for a grandmother or godmother, or even his or her schoolteacher. The words 'TEA TIME' were painted using fingertips, while the corners of the tray were decorated with two bold handprints. Finish a wooden object such as a tray with a couple of coats of water-based acrylic varnish, to seal the paint and protect the design.

little tips

You can find a wide variety of unfired ceramic objects at paint-your-own-china shops. Many shops will be happy for you to purchase an item and decorate it at home, then the shop will fire it for you at a later date.

YOU WILL NEED:
medium-sized potato • star-shaped cookie cutter • chopping board • sharp knife (to be used by an adult only) • kitchen paper or dry cloth • paint in your chosen colours • saucers to hold the paint • plain paper

cut your shape
Cut the potato in half, making sure the surface of the potato is as flat as possible. Place the cookie cutter on a chopping board with the cutting edge facing upwards. Press the potato down on the cutter. Cut away the excess potato using a sharp knife.

dip in paint
If the potato is particularly wet, blot it on kitchen paper or a dry cloth. Pour out the paint into different saucers. Dip the potato into the paint, making sure that the whole shape is covered in paint.

get printing
Begin printing with the potato on the plain paper. To ensure the whole design prints properly, show the child how to use a gentle rocking motion, moving the potato from side to side without lifting it from the paper. This will help to apply the paint evenly, even if the potato is not completely flat.

add more colours
If you wish to add more colours, wash or wipe the paint off the potato and allow it to dry. (It may be quicker to simply cut another design from the remaining half of the potato.) Continue printing in another colour, then allow the design to dry.

Potato printing is a traditional technique that is a favourite with children of all ages – and it's very inexpensive too! You can experiment with other fruit and vegetables, including apples, rhubarb and pears. The potatoes can be cut using cookie cutters, or an adult could use a sharp knife to cut out a few different shapes by hand.

potato printing

wrap it up

We used a simple star shape and printed with red paint on plain white paper to create this festive Christmas wrapping paper. Plain A3-size photocopier paper is perfect for this project.

tea towels

Fruit and vegetable printing works equally well on fabric. We used an apple print in red and green on natural calico for these fun tea towels, which would make a very practical yet pretty gift.

print pictures

Cut large apples in half to print these fun pictures in bold red and fresh green tones. We carefully added the stalk detail using a fine paintbrush. The prints were placed in frames painted in contrasting colours before hanging them on the wall.

little tips

If you are potato-printing on fabric, make sure that you use fabric or stencil paint, so the item can be washed • Take note of the manufacturer's instructions on how to make the paint 'fix' – some paint needs be fixed with a hot iron.

This is a perfect project for toddlers, who will be fascinated by the process. You may have to do the painting in stages – for example, the lion's face first, then the mane – otherwise the paint dries too quickly.

mirror-image painting

YOU WILL NEED:
plain paper • pencil • paint in your chosen colours • paintbrushes in various sizes • saucers to hold the paint • small pompom for lion's nose, if required

fold paper in half Fold the paper in half, pressing down flat to form a crease. Open up the paper and draw a semicircle on one side of the paper in pencil (you may like to use a plate to draw a more accurate circle).

start painting Fill in the semicircle with paint. It is important to do this fairly quickly, or the paint will start to dry and will not transfer properly to the other side of the paper when it is folded.

fold over Fold the paper in half on the original crease and press down firmly. Open the paper to reveal the mirror image of the face. The next stage is the lion's mane – again, it may be easier to draw this before painting. Fill in the triangles with paint, fold the paper in half, and open up to reveal the mane.

finish off Fill in one eye and half of the mouth using brown paint. Fold the paper in half, press it flat and open to reveal the face of the lion. As a finishing touch, we added a small pompom for the lion's nose.

YOU WILL NEED:

paint in your chosen colours •
paintbrushes in various sizes •
saucers to hold the paint • one
large stone for the body • two
small round stones for the eyes •
two flat oval-shaped stones for
the feet • strong glue

paint stones Paint the large stone for the body green all over and allow to dry. For the best results, apply a second coat and let dry. We painted the top of the stone first, then the underside when the top was completely dry. Paint the smaller stones green, and let dry.

add the details Paint on the spots using a darker shade of green paint. If you want very regular spots, draw them on the stone first, using a pencil. Fill in the spots using a finer paintbrush. Now use a fine paintbrush and white paint to paint on the frog's mouth.

paint eyes and feet Paint the small round stones for the eyes with a circle of white paint for the frog's eyes, then leave to dry. Now, using a finer paintbrush, paint on the black eyeballs. Decorate the flatter oval stones for the frog's feet with dark green spots to match the body.

finish off Use strong glue to fix the frog's eyes to the top of the body. Repeat for the feet on the underside of the stone. Allow to dry completely.

Painted stones can be used to create a variety of items, such as paperweights, jewellery and bookends. The shape of the stone may inspire its design – ask your child what the stone looks like, and what they think it could be made into.

painted stones

friendship stones

These pretty friendship stones have been decorated with simple flower motifs, allowing the natural colours of the stone to show through. Use a pencil to write your friend's name or a message on the underside of the stone.

frog bookend

One large stone and four smaller stones were used to create this handsome frog bookend (see pages 20–21 for the full technique). You could make a pair of them to sit on a bookshelf to support your books.

ladybird paperweight

To create these cute little paperweights, use bright red paint to cover stones of various different sizes. Use a finer paintbrush to add the ladybird markings in black, then dab on tiny white dots to depict the eyes.

little tips

It is important to remember that is illegal to remove stones from beaches in certain countries • Garden centres sell bags of stones in assorted sizes • You may like to finish stones with a couple of coats of water-based acrylic varnish to seal the paint when the projects are finished. Allow the varnish to dry completely between coats.

Stencilling can be used to decorate many items – paper, card, wood and fabric. You can buy cardboard or plastic stencils, both of which are easy to use. Single stencils are better for younger children, who may be confused by repeat patterns, as they are quite tricky to position correctly.

stencilling

position the stencil

Place the stencil onto the apron in the position to be stencilled. Use pieces of masking tape on each corner to hold the stencil securely in place. It is important that the stencil is not moved during the stencilling process, as this will cause the design to smudge.

YOU WILL NEED:

apron or other object to be decorated • stencil • masking tape • saucers to hold the paint • fabric paint in your chosen colours • stubby stencil brush • cloth or kitchen paper

apply the paint

Dip the stencilling brush into the paint and remove as much excess paint as possible by wiping it on a cloth or kitchen paper. If there is too much paint on the brush, it will leak through the edges of the stencil and the outline may 'bleed'. Allow the paint to dry slightly before removing the stencil.

remove the stencil

When the paint is dry (or almost dry), peel off the masking tape and lift the stencil to reveal the design. Repeat patterns usually have markings at the corners to help you get the spacing right, so make sure you have marked these before taking off the stencil.

repeat the pattern

Place the stencil in the correct position and repeat the design, first removing any excess paint on a cloth or kitchen paper. When you have finished and the apron is dry, fix the fabric paint with a hot iron, as per the manufacturer's instructions.

aprons and tea towels

These simple aprons are made in natural unbleached calico edged in red and pink bias binding. We used a simple heart-shaped stencil to decorate the edges of the red apron, while the pink apron features a fun cookie stencil, which is a two-part design stencilled in beige with pink icing. See pages 24–25 for the full technique.

decorated box

Boys will love keeping their special treasures in this hand-painted wooden box. We applied two coats of pale blue paint to the box, letting it dry thoroughly between coats. Next, we decorated the box using a traditional toy-soldier stencil in bold dark blue paint, which really stands out on the light blue background. The soldier design is also repeated on the lid of the box. To finish, we applied a couple of coats of water-based acrylic varnish, which seals the paint and protects the design.

little tips

Young children are not renowned for their patience, and waiting for paint to dry is difficult. Have a hairdryer to hand, so that the paint can be quickly dried on a warm setting (but keep it out of the reach of children, as hairdryers are a fire hazard) • If you are making a gift, always practise the technique first on paper.

fabric

Weaving is fun for most ages except the very young. The technique is easy to accomplish and can be applied to both two- and three-dimensional projects. Children will love making cushions and bags from woven ribbons, as well as pen pots or boxes using coloured pipe-cleaners.

weaving

YOU WILL NEED:
four spools of different coloured ribbon, each one approximately 2cm wide • pins • square of fabric approximately 45cm x 45cm • needle and thread • scissors

cut the ribbon Cut the ribbon into 45cm lengths and divide into separate piles by colour for easier selection when weaving. We used brightly coloured satin ribbons, although you could substitute pretty pastels or even lengths of fabric cut with pinking shears.

pin along edge Carefully arrange the ribbon lengths down one side of the fabric square, alternating two different colours. Pin the ribbons in place using one pin per length of ribbon to hold them firmly in place during weaving.

start weaving Take one of the remaining ribbon pieces and pin it to the adjacent side of the fabric square. Thread the ribbon over the first piece of ribbon and under the next and repeat until you reach the other side of the fabric square. Pin the ribbon in place. Repeat with the other ribbon colour until the weaving is finished. Pin each piece of ribbon in place to stop it from slipping.

stitch to base Use a needle and thread to tack neatly around the four sides of the weaving, stitching the ribbons to the fabric square.

pen and pencil holder

Use the same weaving technique using coloured pipe-cleaners and fold the finished product around an empty can or jar to create this fun pencil holder. The ends of the pipe-cleaners are folded over inside the can and they are folded flat at the bottom. To finish, twist the ends of the pipe-cleaners together and trim the edges with scissors.

bag

This fun bag is made using the same technique as shown on pages 30–31, but using satin and velvet ribbons in different widths. The bag is backed in plain cotton and the strap is made using two lengths of ribbon in different colours. To finish, we added a cute little butterfly made from twisted pipe-cleaners.

cushion

To make the woven ribbon into a cushion cover, cut another fabric square measuring 45cm x 45cm. With the right sides facing, stitch the two pieces together on three sides. Turn right side out, insert a cushion pad, and hand-stitch the opening closed. Alternatively, you could press the ribbon edges under and stitch the weaving to a ready-made cushion cover. A pretty wool flower corsage adds the finishing touch.

little tips

With younger children, try weaving strips of coloured paper and glue the edges in place • Fabric scraps can be substituted for ribbons, but it is important to trim the edges with pinking shears to prevent them from fraying.

Even younger children will enjoy making these animal finger puppets from felt. Very young children can glue rather than stitch them, as this eliminates the problem of sharp needles. Look through picture books for other ideas, and ask your child to draw any other animals he or she would like to make.

finger puppets

pin and cut out
Trace the templates on page 119 onto paper and cut them out. Pin the templates to the felt. Carefully cut out the felt. You will need two body shapes per puppet. We used pinking shears to cut out the bodies, but normal scissors will do, as felt does not fray.

sew body pieces together
Holding two body pieces together, hand-stitch around the edges using a running stitch in matching thread. Leave the bottom section open. If younger children are unable to sew, the edges can be glued together. When making the sheep puppet, fold a pleat in the base of the two ear shapes (as shown on the template) and tuck the ends of the ears inside the body sections before stitching in place.

glue on the heads
For the lion puppet, apply neat dots of glue to the back of the mane and carefully place it on the front of the finger puppet. Push down firmly, then allow to dry completely. For the sheep puppet, glue on the little white face section and allow to dry.

finish off
Use three-dimensional fabric paint to carefully draw the nose and eyes onto the finger puppets. Allow to dry completely.

YOU WILL NEED:
cardboard for pompom discs • pencil • scissors • assorted balls of wool

wind the wool Trace the pompom disc template on page 118 onto paper and cut it out. Place it on a piece of cardboard and draw round it. Repeat. Cut out two discs. Start to wind wool around the two discs. When the first ball of wool is finished, tie the end of the ball to the beginning of a new one. Wind the wool round the disc until it is completely covered.

cut around the outside When the winding process is complete, hold the pompom discs securely, then cut around the edges of the wool using scissors. The wool will come away and look like fringing at this point, and it is important that the two discs are firmly held together.

secure the wool Cut two lengths of wool approximately 20cm long and thread between the two cardboard discs. Pull together tightly and tie in a knot. It is a good idea to tie several knots so that the wool is very secure.

pull apart and finish off Gently pull away the cardboard discs from the pompom. If it proves difficult, just cut them off. Trim any excess bits of wool and fluff the pompom ball to give it a nice round shape.

pompoms

Old-fashioned pompoms are so easy to make and are a great way of using up left-over wool. They can be made in a variety of sizes and used to create toys, including cute kittens and fluffy chicks for Easter, as well as fun jewellery and decorations for bags and cushions.

pompom kittycats

These cute little cats are made using two different-sized pompoms made from the same dark grey wool. Use the ends of the pompom ties to join the two pompoms together before trimming the ends. We added little ears snipped from a piece of grey felt, some black wool whiskers and a little grey wool tail to finish.

cream

cushion

These fun cushions are made from coloured wool fabric with felt petals stitched to one corner to form a simple flower motif. We added contrastingly coloured pompoms to the centre of the flowers to give the cushions an interesting three-dimensional design.

flower bag

A pompom forms the centre of a bold flower that decorates a pretty handmade bag made from coloured wool fabric. Use two rectangles of fabric to make the bag. Place the fabric right sides together and stitch around three sides, leaving one shorter end open. Finish the handles with neat blanket stitch. Sew five fabric petals to one side of the bag, and finish the flower by stitching a pompom to the centre.

little tips

Try making pompoms using different coloured wools combined together, which gives a fun multicolour effect • Remember that the more times the wool is wrapped around the disc, the fuller and bouncier the finished pompom will be.

These simple heart-shaped lavender bags make great gifts and are very easy to make. Use coloured felt or scraps of cotton cut with pinking shears to prevent the fabric from fraying. Fill them with dried lavender and decorate with ribbons, buttons and bows to finish.

lavender pockets

YOU WILL NEED:
plain paper • scissors • pins •
coloured felt squares or scraps
of cotton fabric • pinking
shears • needle • embroidery
thread • loose dried lavender •
button • 20cm of narrow
ribbon

pin in position Trace the
heart template on page 118 onto a
piece of plain paper and cut it out.
Lay two pieces of felt or cotton fabric
on top of one another, and pin the
heart template to the fabric.

cut out Using the pinking shears, carefully cut all the way
around the heart template, making sure you are cutting
neatly through both layers of fabric. The pinking shears give
an attractive zig-zag effect to the edge of the fabric, which
also stops it from fraying and means it doesn't have to be
hemmed. If you are making more than one lavender heart,
it's a good idea to cut them all out at the same time.

stitch Thread the needle with the embroidery thread (use a short piece of
thread, as longer lengths can get tangled, which is very frustrating). Start a
simple running stitch at the bottom point of the heart and continue all the way
around the heart, leaving an opening of around 4cm.

fill and finish off Fill the
heart with lavender before continuing
the stitching to close the heart. Using
20cm of narrow ribbon, make a
hanging loop and stitch it to the
centre of the heart. Glue on a button
to cover the ends of the ribbon.

YOU WILL NEED:
sheet card 50cm square • blue
cotton 60cm x 60cm • green
cotton 60cm x 30cm • other
coloured cotton fabrics • felt • fur
fabric • pompoms • lolly sticks •
glue • scissors • pinking shears •
paint • saucer to hold paint •
fine paintbrushes

select materials Assemble
the fabrics together with the paint
and lolly sticks. Glue the pale blue
cotton to the cardboard. Cut out the
grass from green fabric (we used
pinking shears to prevent the fabric
from fraying). Glue the grass section
in place and allow to dry.

cut out shapes Carefully cut out two tree and two
cloud shapes from the felt. Cut three sheep shapes from the
fur fabric, and assorted flower and fruit shapes from the
coloured cotton. Children may find it easier to draw the
shapes on the back of the fabric with felt-tip pen before they
cut them out.

place and glue shapes Once the pieces are cut out, they can be
laid out on the background fabric. Your child may like to experiment with them
first to see where the pieces look best. Once he or she has decided where to put
each piece, they can be glued in place. Allow the glue to dry.

add details Cut out stem shapes
in felt, and glue in place. Cut the lolly
sticks in half to form the uprights of the
fence and glue. Use whole lollipop sticks
for the horizontal bars and glue in place.
Glue on the pompoms for the bunny
and add ears. Paint in the birds in the
sky and the flower centres.

Collage is enjoyed by children of all ages. Use ready-cut felt pieces for small children, who will enjoy simply glueing the shapes in place. Older children will relish cutting out their own shapes and embellishing their collages with paint, sequins and beads.

fabric collage

wallhanging

Fabric collages make ideal
wallhangings. Here, a lively
country scene (see pages 42–43
for the full technique) makes a
pretty wallhanging for a child's
bedroom. A farmyard scene or a
row of cottages would work
equally well. Hang the collage
from a length of ribbon glued or
stapled to the back of the collage.

tea cosy

You can use bondaweb or another fusible web to create fabric collages that can be machine-washed. This decorative floral tea cosy features a teacup and saucer design that has been applied to the fabric using iron-on bondaweb and finished with blanket stitch and a cute spotted ribbon bow.

t-shirt

To decorate this T-shirt with a cupcake motif, we used cotton fabric backed in bondaweb. Draw a cupcake motif onto paper, then cut out a template. Pin this to your chosen fabrics, cut out the cupcake shape, and attach to the front of the T-shirt using bondaweb and following the manufacturer's instructions. We added tiny red beads as a finishing touch.

little tips

Create a collage box and save lengths of ribbon, lollipop sticks, pieces of foil, cardboard and anything you think might come in useful for creating collages · This collage method works equally well with just paper and cardboard, which is much easier for younger children to cut out and glue.

tie-dye

Tie-dyeing is a simple process with striking results. You can give old white T-shirts a new lease of life with this technique, but it is is advisable to have an adult on hand during the actual dyeing process, as it can get quite messy. Alternatively, you can follow the steps shown here to create the design, but use machine dye rather than the bucket method, as it's an easier (and less messy) option.

YOU WILL NEED:
t-shirt • string • dye in the colour of your choice • scissors • bucket • jug • wooden spoon

tie up material
Tie the string around the sleeves of the T-shirt in two places and pull tightly to ensure no dye can get through. Repeat on the body of the T-shirt, tying two pieces of string at 10cm intervals. If you want additional stripes, tie more lengths of string around the T-shirt.

place item in dye
Following the manufacturer's instructions, make up the dye in a bucket, adding dye fix if necessary. Push the T-shirt into the bucket of dye and stir gently with a wooden spoon to ensure the fabric is evenly covered with the dye. Leave the T-shirt for approximately one hour, stirring occasionally.

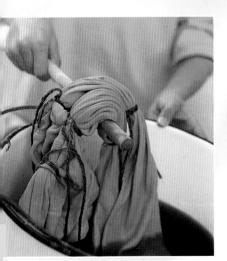

remove the t-shirt
When the dye process is complete, carefully remove the T-shirt from the bucket and wash the items according to the dye manufacturer's instructions. Leave the strings in place on the T-shirt.

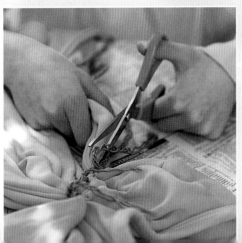

cut the strings
Allow the T-shirt to dry completely. Use a pair of scissors to carefully cut the strings, taking care not to damage the T-shirt. Iron the T-shirt to remove the crease marks left by the string.

paper

paper flowers

Paper flowers are quick and easy to make and are a great way of using up old wrapping paper and tissue. Use pipe-cleaners or drinking straws to make stems, then stand the flowers in vases made from plastic cups covered in tissue paper. Alternatively, use the flowers to make pretty jewellery or to decorate handmade cards.

YOU WILL NEED:
paper for flower template • pencil • scissors • coloured card for the main flower shape and the flower centres• coloured tissue paper or crêpe paper • stick of glue • pipe-cleaners for the flower stems • sticky tape

draw out flower Trace the flower template on page 118 onto paper and cut out with scissors. Draw around the template on coloured card and cut out the flower shape carefully.

cut out petals Trace the petal template shown on page 118 and use it to cut five petals from crêpe paper or tissue paper. You can layer the flowers by cutting out five additional petals, which can be glued on top of the first petals to create a fuller effect.

glue on petals Fold a small pleat in the bottom end of each petal. Apply glue to the back of a petal and stick it to the centre of the card flower. Repeat for each petal, allowing the glue to dry completely.

finish off Cut out a small circle of card, approximately 1.5cm in diameter, and glue it to the centre of the flower to cover the ends of the petals. Use a small piece of sticky tape to attach a pipe-cleaner to the back of the flower to form a stem.

hair decoration

This pretty paper flower was cut from cardboard and adorned with crêpe-paper petals using the technique shown on pages 50–51. The finished flower was then glued to a sturdy hairclip.

greeting card

Glue two crêpe-paper flowers to a plain card to create a decorative three-dimensional card that's perfect for birthdays or Mother's Day.

brooch

This brooch was made from cardboard and crêpe paper. Cut a circle of cardboard approximately 3cm in diameter. Cut out six large crêpe-paper petals and six smaller crêpe-paper petals in two different colours. Glue a circle of large petals to the cardboard, and then a circle of small petals. Finish off with a pompom.

little tips

If you are using tissue paper or crêpe paper to make the flower petals, be sure to use stick glue rather than PVA glue, as the latter will make the paper dissolve.

Create fans using brightly coloured and decorative paper – sheets of wrapping paper are a perfect choice. Finished off with long silk tassels, paper fans are quick and easy to make, and are a great addition to the dressing-up box.

fan making

YOU WILL NEED:
coloured paper or wrapping
paper • scissors • glue • glitter
• silk tassels • stapler

cut out To make a paper fan,
cut a piece of paper measuring
approximately 50cm x 25cm.

fold paper Place the sheet of paper flat on the table
with the shortest edge in front of you. Starting at the end
closest to you, make even folds that are approximately 2cm
wide, turning the paper over each time to create a pleated
effect. Press each fold flat (you could use a ruler to rub over
the fold to make it as flat as possible).

decorate To decorate the fan, open out the pleats slightly and use glue to
create a swirling pattern along the top edge of the paper. Scatter glitter over
the glue and shake to remove the excess. Allow the glue to dry thoroughly
before folding up the fan again.

finish off Pinch the pleats at the
bottom of the fan firmly together, and
insert the top of the silk tassel in
between the central pleats. Use a
stapler to secure the pleats (two or
three staples are usually sufficient). If
children are very young, an adult
should be responsible for the stapling.

Boys and girls alike will delight in making these colourful windmills that twirl in the wind. Try making extra ones and stand them in flowerpots for fun party decorations.

paper windmills

YOU WILL NEED:
two different-coloured squares of paper measuring 20cm x 20cm • glue • scissors • card for the circular centre • pins • small piece of cork • stick approximately 30cm in length

choose colours Choose the colours of paper you are going to use to make the windmill. We used bold green, blue and yellow, but soft pastels or hot pink and zingy orange look great too.

glue and cut Apply a thin layer of glue all over the back of one sheet of paper. Carefully lay the other sheet on top and press flat. Rub firmly, making sure there are no wrinkles or air bubbles trapped between the two sheets. Allow the glue to dry completely. Now, from the corner of each square, cut a line approximately 10cm long towards to the centre of the paper.

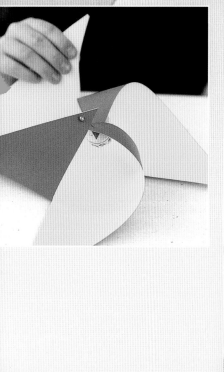

form blades With the square of paper in front of you, gently bend every other point of the paper back along the cut line and into the centre. Hold in place with your fingers and draw in the next corner. Repeat until all four corners are folded into the centre.

secure with pin Push a pin through the centre, making sure it goes through all four corners. It is advisable for an adult to do this. Push the pin into a cork. Using strong glue, attach the stick to the back of the cork, and allow the glue to dry. Glue a disc of card on to conceal the pin, if desired.

YOU WILL NEED:
paper for template • pencil • scissors • thin card in assorted colours • glue • sharp blade to cut holes for pins (to be used by an adult) • split pins (available from most stationers)

cut out Trace the teddy templates on page 121 onto plain paper and cut them out. Draw around the templates on a piece of card and cut them out. You will need twelve identical-sized ovals to make up the teddy's legs, arms and ears, then one each for the nose, head and body. We used a contrastingly coloured piece of card for the teddy's nose.

glue on nose Use glue to stick the nose to the teddy's face and allow it to dry completely. Lay out all the pieces of the teddy bear on a table so you can work out where the positions for the holes should be.

mark and cut holes Use a pencil to mark the holes for the pins and make sure that each of the card sections overlaps at this point, so they will be held together by the pins. Use a sharp blade to make slits through the layers of card. It is advisable for an adult to do this, as blades are dangerous.

insert the split pins Insert the split pins through each slit and fold them flat at the back of the bear. Continue until the whole teddy has been assembled. We added a decorative pin through the teddy's nose as a finishing touch.

Split-pin animals are fun to make and educational, too, as they teach young children about joints and movement. As you cut out and make them, describe how the sections will move when held together by the split pins. The pins can also be used decoratively to make buttons and eyes.

split-pin animals

little bunnies

Use the templates on page 120 to create these cute split-pin bunnies. We used card in two shades of pink and attached the finished bunnies to a length of ribbon with miniature wooden pegs to create a fun decoration for a child's room.

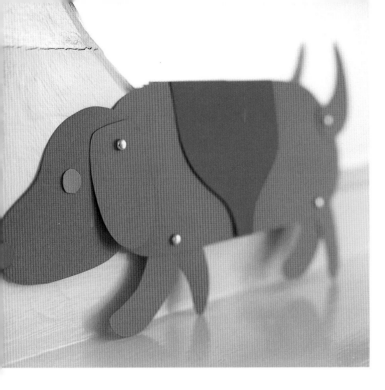

sausage dog

This colourful sausage dog can be made using the templates on pages 120–121 and by following the instructions on pages 58–59. The dog can be created in any length – simply elongate the body template. The dog's legs and tail are made from the same template. Add a fabric jacket to ring the changes.

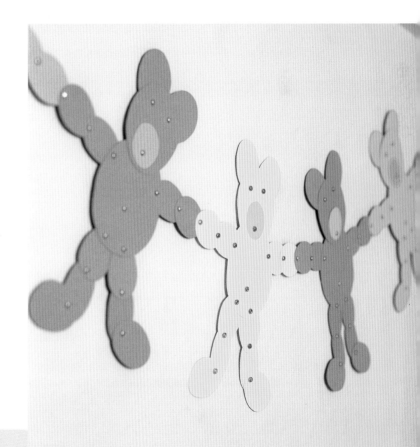

teddy garland

Using the technique shown on pages 58–59, we made a series of cheerful teddy bears in cool greens, yellows and blue. The teddies are strung together by their paws using split pins, then used to decorate a plain wall.

little tips

Try decorating the cardboard sections with colourful glitter or painted decorations before joining them together with the split pins. Decorating their creations will keep the kids happily occupied for even longer!

paper chains

Traditional paper chains are so easy to make, and look fantastic at children's parties or other celebrations. We used a combination of zingy hot pinks and oranges, but you could try making paper chains in soft pastel tones or in red and white for Christmas decorations.

YOU WILL NEED:
selection of coloured paper at least 28cm wide • pencil • ruler • scissors • glue

choose colours Ask your child what colours she or he would like to use to create the chains. For more decorative paper chains, you could use patterned wrapping paper or translucent tracing paper, which is available from art shops in a variety of different colours.

draw strips Using a pencil and ruler, draw the strips on the back of the paper, making sure that each one is approximately 2cm wide. From an A4-sized sheet of paper (if used landscape), you should get around fourteen strips.

cut strips Using scissors, cut out the strips. It is a good idea to keep the colours separate by making a pile of strips in each colour, so they are easier to select when joining the chains together.

glue strips into chains Form a loop with the first paper chain and put a dab of glue on one end to fix it together. For the next link in the chain, thread the paper through the loop and glue the ends. Repeat for each link until you have made the required length of paper chain.

Use pretty handmade paper to cover textbooks or notebooks. You can use them at school or give them as gifts. The same technique can be used to decorate boxes or photo albums, which make welcome keepsakes.

covering books

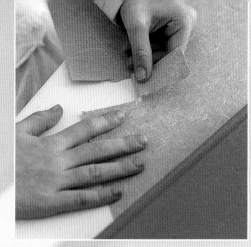

YOU WILL NEED:
selection of decorative papers • scissors • glue • books to cover • pencil • fine paintbrush, if necessary

cut out paper Lay the book out flat on the paper to be used to cover it. Cut around the book, leaving a margin of approximately 4cm of extra paper around all the sides. Where the spine of the book lies, cut two slits in the paper at the top and bottom of the book, and fold them inwards to hide them.

glue on cover Fold the remaining edges of the paper toward the inside of the book and make pleated folds at the corners to neaten the edges. Glue the paper in place and allow to dry completely. It is a good idea to glue each layer of paper at the folded corners so that they stay in place.

cut out decorations Use scissors to cut out a selection of flowers, petals and whatever other decorations are desired. These can be drawn using a pencil first, or cut out freehand, depending on the child.

decorate Lay out the paper shapes on the book to create the design. When you are happy with the arrangement, glue each piece in place. If the pieces are very small, it is a good idea to use a fine paintbrush to apply the glue to the back of the paper. Allow to dry thoroughly.

gift boxes

Use ready-made gift boxes or recycle
chocolate and biscuit boxes to create
these pretty gifts. Cover the boxes in
paper, then cut out heart and flower
petals in contrasting colours and
differently textured paper to decorate
the box with. If desired, you could use
the template for a paper flower given
on page 118.

photo album

To make this album, use two stiff pieces of card covered in paper. The word 'PHOTOS' and a flower in paper were then glued to the front. Insert paper inside the two layers of card and use a hole punch to make holes through the card and paper. Thread with narrow elastic to hold together and finish with a ribbon bow.

books

Decorative flowers, or narrow strips of coloured paper glued in horizontal bands, look great on paper-covered books. Boys can decorate their books with boats, trains or car shapes cut from brightly coloured papers.

little tips

Remember that the thinner the paper, the easier it will be to cover items. Thick handmade paper can be quite difficult to fold, particularly at the corners. It's best to save thicker handmade papers for the decorations, as they will be easier to glue to the flat surfaces of the objects.

Like paper chains, paper lanterns are a traditional and fun way of using paper to make three-dimensional objects. They look great strung across a window or mantelpiece. We decorated ours with bands of gingham ribbon, but you could substitute buttons, sequins or glitter.

paper lanterns

YOU WILL NEED:
sheets of A4 paper in various
colours • scissors • glue •
ribbon to decorate

cut and fold paper Cut a
strip of paper approximately 1cm
wide from the shortest side of the
piece of paper and set aside. This will
make the hanging loop. Now, cut a
square 20cm x 20cm. Fold the square
in half and press flat.

cut equal strips Cutting inwards from the folded
edge of the paper, use scissors to snip flaps that finish
approximately 3cm from the top of the paper. Each flap
should be spaced about 2cm apart. You may want to mark
these lines out using a pencil and a ruler first, to make it
easier for the child to cut the paper properly.

glue into round To make the lantern shape, unfold the creased edge
and roll the paper to form a tube shape with the paper slits standing vertically.
Glue the edges of the paper together to form a round lantern, then press
downwards gently to form a splayed lantern shape.

finish off Cut a length of ribbon to
fit around the top of the lantern and
glue in place. Glue the ends of the
hanging loop to the top of the lantern
on both sides, and allow to dry
completely.

This very effective paper technique will provide children with hours of pleasure and can be adapted to suit most ages. Collect wrapping paper, paper doilies, newspapers and magazine cuttings and keep in a special découpage box. You can also buy books of découpage scraps.

découpage

tear and cut materials

Découpage looks particularly effective when both cut and torn pieces of paper are used – the ragged edges add to the layered effect. For added interest, you could also try using decorative scissors and pinking shears to cut some of the paper.

glue on Start by sticking on larger pieces of paper to cover the box completely. This saves time and provides a good background for the smaller pieces of paper that are added later. Always allow the glue to dry thoroughly before embarking on the next layer of paper.

layer upon layer When the first layer is dry, add further smaller pieces of paper. We used torn pieces of paper as well as smaller squares to cover the box. Try to allow some drying time between layers, so that the wet glue does not cause the layer beneath to peel away.

finish off Finish the découpage with smaller shapes such as flowers or leaves cut from wrapping paper. It may be easier to use a fine paintbrush to apply the glue to these smaller, more fiddly pieces of paper.

toy-box

Simple black-and-white designs look particularly effective in découpage. This toy-box was made from an old shoe box, and has been covered with designs of antique playing cards photocopied from a non-copyright book on the subject.

craft kit

Layers of handmade papers decorated with floral and metallic designs were used to cover this craft kit box. Individual flowers and leaf shapes were cut out to finish off the découpage design.

bon-bon box

Layers of handmade paper and roses cut from scraps of vintage-style wallpaper were used to cover a heart-shaped box, which was then filled with sweets to create a pretty gift for a friend or relative. The edges are trimmed with paper lace cut from the edge of a rectangular doily and finished with a border of thin velvet ribbon.

little tips

Découpage is traditionally finished with layers of varnish to make the object more durable. A few layers of water-based acrylic varnish is ideal, but make sure that it is applied in thin layers to prevent saturating the paper, which could peel off. Allow the varnish to dry thoroughly between each coat.

modelling

papier mâché dinosaur

Papier mâché is a really hands-on messy project, so make sure you have enough time to get the materials ready and to clear up afterwards! Kids love working with papier mâché due to its sloshy consistency and the fact it can be used to create fantastic three-dimensional objects.

YOU WILL NEED:
newspaper • balloon • bowl to
support balloon • thick
brushes • PVA glue • bowl for
glue • aluminium foil for the
dinosaur's legs and head •
cardboard (we used the back of
a hard-backed envelope) •
paint • masking tape

cover balloon Tear the
newspaper into strips and put aside.
Blow up the balloon and balance it on
a bowl while sticking on the paper.
Using a brush, apply glue to the
balloon. Cover with paper. Repeat the
process, building up layers of paper,
until the balloon is thickly covered.

add legs and head We used ordinary aluminium
foil rolled into short cylinder shapes for the legs and head.
Use masking tape to fix them to the balloon. Apply glue to
the legs and head and cover with strips of paper. Make sure
that the strips overlap onto the body so that the head and
legs will be securely held in place once the glue has dried.

add spines Cut out triangles approximately 2cm wide and 4cm high from
the cardboard. Fold the bottom of the triangle at a ninety-degree angle and
glue the flat part to the balloon. Form two lines to create the dinosaur's spikes.
When the glue is dry, apply another layer of paper to hold the spikes in place.

finish off Once the glue is dry, the
dinosaur is ready to paint. It is best to
leave the papier mâché overnight to
make sure all the layers are dry. Paint
the dinosaur body in mauve and the
spikes in bright blue. Allow the paint
to dry completely. We added blue spots
to the body to finish off.

YOU WILL NEED:
**balsa wood in assorted lengths
and thicknesses (most craft or
modelling shops sell packs of
balsa wood) • glue • paint •
paintbrushes in various sizes •
saucers to hold the paint •
scissors • scraps of fabric for sail**

glue base

Cut seven lengths of balsa wood measuring 10cm x 1cm x 1cm for the base of the boat. Lay two pieces of the wood about 9cm apart and glue the other five pieces on the top at equal intervals. For the mast, cut two squares of wood measuring 1cm x 1cm and two lengths measuring 10cm x 5mm.

paint base

Paint the base of the boat and the mast sections and allow them to dry completely. You may need to apply a further coat of paint to ensure even coverage. Allow the paint to dry completely before attaching the mast.

make sail and mast

Cut out a triangle of fabric about 8cm wide and 8cm high, using pinking shears to prevent the fabric from fraying. Lay one mast piece on the table and apply glue down the centre of the fabric triangle before placing it on the mast. Lay the second mast on top, so the sail is neatly sandwiched between the pieces of wood, then glue in place. Allow to dry.

attach sail

Glue the base of the mast to the two squares of balsa wood so that it is held between them. Now apply a blob of glue to the centre of the boat base, and stick the sail and mast to the base. Allow the glue to dry. You may wish to apply more paint to cover the glue in this area.

Balsa wood is easy to cut and glue, which makes it ideal for children to use for modelling. Small pieces can be cut with scissors, but thicker pieces of balsa wood should be cut by an adult using a junior hacksaw.

modelling with balsa wood

sailing ship

This fun sailing ship was made using the technique shown on pages 78–79. Children will have hours of fun sailing their ships in buckets, the bath, or even a local pond, but do remember to attach a length of string if you're sailing the boat outdoors, so that it can't float away!

doll's table and chairs

You'll need a piece of balsa wood measuring 6cm x 10cm for the top of this table, and four legs made from 1cm-square balsa wood cut into 4cm lengths. The chair seats and legs were made from balsa, while the ladder-style backs were made from lolly sticks. We painted the table blue and added a decorative motif in red to match the colour of the chairs.

doll's bed

A delightful addition to any little girl's doll's house, this bed is made from a piece of balsa measuring approximately 10cm x 6cm wide. The back was cut from a thin piece of balsa wood and the legs are four 1cm-square cubes of balsa wood. The bed was painted red and decorated with a Shaker-style motif in white, done using a fine paintbrush. The quilt was made from two rectangles of gingham fabric trimmed with a length of blue gingham ribbon.

little tips

If you're working with young children, it's advisable to cut the lengths of balsa wood for them. Any rough edges should be lightly sanded with sandpaper to smooth them off. Having pre-cut pieces of balsa means that the kids can move on quickly to the fun bits of the project – the glueing and painting!

Snow shakers make great gifts for friends and family, and children really enjoy making them. We used Christmas decorations inside ours, but your child may like to use small plastic animals or to make their own decorations to put inside.

snow shakers

YOU WILL NEED:
empty, clean jam jars •
distilled water • glycerine •
liquid detergent • jug and
spoon for pouring • glitter •
Christmas decorations to put
in jar • strong waterproof glue

fill jars Use a jug to pour the distilled water into the jam jar. Fill it as full as possible. Add two teaspoons of glycerine, and half a teaspoon of detergent.

add glitter Spoon the glitter into the water. You will need approximately five or six teaspoons. White or silver glitter looks most similar to snow, although red or green or other bright colours can look very festive.

attach decoration Use a blob of strong waterproof glue to securely stick the decoration to the inside of the jam-jar lid. It is advisable for an adult to do this if the child is young. Allow the glue to dry thoroughly according to the manufacturer's instructions.

secure lid Carefully place the lid on the top of the jam jar and screw tightly in place. The jam jar should be watertight, but you may wish to seal it around the edges with a layer of craft silicone sealant, which is available from good craft shops.

YOU WILL NEED:
air-drying modelling clay • rolling pin • assorted cookie cutters • spatula • paint dish or saucer • paintbrushes • paint • glue • loose sequins • tweezers • drinking straw • self-adhesive magnets • ribbon for necklaces • metal pins for brooches

roll out Remove the clay from its packaging and knead to soften it. Roll the clay out with a rolling pin. For smaller objects such as brooches, the clay should be about 5mm thick. For larger objects, the clay should be about 8mm thick.

cut out Use assorted cookie cutters to cut the shapes from the clay. Carefully remove the excess clay from around the cutter before removing it. Use a spatula to lift the clay shape and place on a tray to allow it to dry. When the top is dry, turn the shape over so the other side can dry completely.

paint and decorate Paint your clay shapes using brightly coloured paints. You will probably need two or three layers of paint to achieve total coverage, but remember to allow each layer to dry thoroughly between coats. Paler colours may need more coats than darker shades.

finish off Decorate the finished clay shapes with sequins or smaller clay shapes using a tiny bit of glue. You may need tweezers to position sequins on the shapes. Stick magnets to the back for fridge magnets, and metal pins to make brooches. Use self-adhesive pads to stick the letters to a door.

Children love working with clay, and it can be used to create fun jewellery for friends, alphabet letters for doors, and funky fridge magnets. Nowadays, metal or plastic cookie cutters come in all sorts of shapes and sizes, and cut clay quickly and easily. Once dry, your clay shapes can be colourfully painted and decorated.

modelling with clay

letter shapes

Children will love cutting out their names in clay letters and sticking them on their bedroom doors. We decorated these letters with tiny flowers, using a miniature cutter for the flower shape and a straw to imprint the central circle in the flower. Paint the letters in bold colours and use self-adhesive pads to attach them to the door. They can also be used to decorate toy-boxes and wooden trunks.

jewellery

Little girls will enjoy creating jewellery for themselves and their friends. Use small cookie-cutter shapes such as flowers and hearts and roll out the clay to 5mm thick, so the shapes are not too heavy. Use the end of a straw to pierce a ribbon hole for necklaces. Paint the shapes in bright colours and decorate with sequins.

fridge magnets

Cookie cutters in the shape of fish, flowers and butterflies can be used to create fun fridge magnets. Paint them in pretty colours and decorate with sequins. Alternatively, use different coloured paint to decorate. Most craft shops now sell self-adhesive magnets that can be bought in strips and cut to size.

little tips

Avoid putting the clay near water, as it will make it sticky and difficult to use • Keep left-over clay wrapped in plastic or in an airtight container for future use • A couple of coats of varnish (applied by an adult) will give the painted clay a longer life.

These classic puppet people have been made by children for years and will provide hours of entertainment. Their outfits are made from semicircles of fabric or paper, while string or wool is used for the hair. We used a large cardboard box covered in wrapping paper to create the puppet theatre.

wooden-spoon puppets

YOU WILL NEED:

wooden spoons • black pen • scissors • string or wool • glue • 30cm dinner plate as template for clothes • pinking shears • cotton fabric, felt or paper doilies for clothes • buttons, ribbons and small silk flowers for decoration

making faces Use a fine liner pen to draw the faces onto the wooden spoons. Let the child use his or her imagination and add rosy cheeks, noses and eyebrows with coloured pencils if they want to.

adding the hair For plaited hair with a fringe, cut six lengths of string or wool measuring approximately 30cm and two lengths measuring 8cm. Knot the shorter pieces of string in the middle of the longer pieces to create the fringe effect. Alternatively, use ten 30cm lengths for long loose hair, and six shorter 6cm lengths for the boy puppet's hair. Glue the hair to the top of the wooden spoon.

dressing up Use a 30cm dinner plate as a template. Place on your chosen fabric and draw round the edge in the black pen. Cut each circle out, then cut into two halves to create semicircular shapes. Use pinking shears to prevent fabric from fraying. Wrap the fabric around the neck of the spoon and glue in place. Add little buttons or ribbons to decorate.

finish off Carefully plait the doll's hair and tie the ends with short lengths of colourful ribbon.

Hanging mobiles are a fun project for boys and girls, and make decorative additions to any bedroom. They are also a lovely present for a new baby. A great variety of materials can be used to make mobiles, from wire and beads to balsa wood and modelling clay.

hanging mobiles

YOU WILL NEED:
wire for the hearts • thinner wire for attaching hearts to mobile • coloured beads • bell for decoration • scissors • two lengths of balsa wood approximately 30cm long • paint for mobile frame • glue

thread beads on wire
Thread the wooden beads onto the wire, alternating the colours for a pretty effect. We used twenty-seven beads for each wired heart.

shape into heart
Place the beaded wire onto a flat surface and bend the wire to form the heart shape. Your child may need a little help in doing this, especially when it comes to forming the loop at the centre.

form loop and make frame
Bend the wire to form a loop in the centre of the heart shape and twist the wire to secure it. Thread the bell onto thin wire and attach to the loop by twisting it around the wire. Now paint the two pieces of balsa wood for the frame. Place one piece on top of the other to form a cross shape, and glue in position.

attach to frame
Cut four 30cm lengths of thin wire and thread one onto each of the heart loops. Twist to secure to the loop, then twist the other end round one end of the frame. Repeat with the other hearts. A dab of glue will hold the wire in place.

cars

Balsa wood is ideal for mobiles, as it is very lightweight and can be easily cut into interesting shapes. For this mobile, we drew little car shapes, wheel shapes and window shapes on thin balsa wood, then cut them out. Paint the cars and windows in bright colours and use black for the wheels. When the paint is dry, glue the windows and wheels onto the car outlines. Make a small hole at the top of each car and thread thin wire through the hole so that it can be attached to the frame.

beaded hearts

This beaded mobile was made using the technique shown on pages 90–91. Threading beads is great for helping children develop their fine motor skills. Younger children who find small beads too fiddly could thread larger beads or painted pasta tubes on shoelaces and suspend them from a mobile frame.

pretty purple flowers

Use a cookie cutter to cut out flower shapes from thinly rolled-out modelling clay, and a drinking straw to cut out a hole to hang them from. Paint the flower shapes both back and front and allow to dry. Then add spots in a contrasting colour. Thread narrow ribbon through each hole and tie a bow. Fix a length of narrow wire to each flower shape, and hang from the mobile frame.

little tips

Look out for small wooden toys or even tiny soft toys to suspend from mobiles for babies • Monochromatic designs in black and white are visually appealing to very young babies, so you could paint bold patterns on clay or wood shapes and paint the bars of the mobile in narrow black and white stripes.

special
occasions

Peg dolls are a traditional craft. They are the perfect size for doll's houses and can be dressed as men or women for this purpose. Peg dolls look delightful dressed as Christmas angels in white lace with silver wings, or as Santa Claus in red felt with a cotton-wool beard.

peg-doll angels

wooden pegs • black pen for face and silver pen for shoes • scraps of lace and cotton for dress • scissors • glue • pipe-cleaner for halo • silver card for wings • sheer ribbon for hanging loop

draw on face and feet

Use the black pen to draw some eyes and mouth on the peg. Colour in the feet to look like shoes using the silver felt-tip pen, and allow to dry.

cut out and glue robes
Cut out a piece of white cotton and a piece of lace both measuring 8cm x 8cm. Lay the white cotton on top of the lace and glue one end of the fabric to the back of the peg doll. Wrap the other layer of fabric around the doll and glue in place at the back.

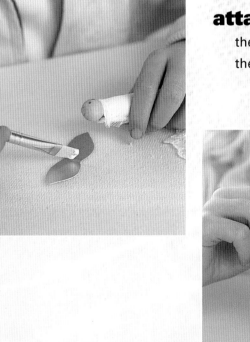

attach wings
Using scissors, carefully cut a pair of small wings from the silver card. Apply a dab of glue to the wings, and stick them into place on the back of the peg doll.

add halo and ribbon
Twist the pipe-cleaner into a circular shape to form a halo, and place it on the peg doll's head. Cut a length of sheer ribbon approximately 20cm long and tie it around the peg doll's neck. Tie the two ends of the ribbon into a knot to form a hanging loop.

YOU WILL NEED:
paper • pencil • scissors

fold paper Take a square piece of paper. Fold it in half diagonally. Fold the paper in half again, and then into quarters. You should now have a small folded paper triangle.

draw on design Using the pencil, draw triangular or scalloped shapes on the folded edges of the paper. You can draw curved shapes on the top edges of the paper (furthest from the centre of the paper), too. Experiment with different shapes, so that all your snowflakes are different.

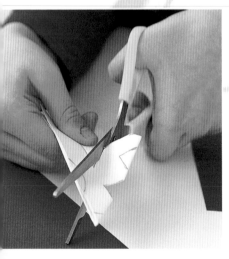

cut out Using the scissors, carefully cut along the lines you have drawn on the paper. Remember that the more shapes you cut out, the more decorative and delicate the snowflake will appear.

pull open Gently unfold the paper and carefully press flat to reveal the snowflake's design. You can cut snowflakes from any size paper, but good sizes are approximately 20cm square for a large snowflake and 10cm square for a small one.

paper snowflakes

**Paper snowflakes are so simple to
make, yet so effective. At Christmas,
use them to decorate windows, stick
them to the wall in a circular shape to
create a wreath effect, or hang them
from bare branches as a tabletop
decoration. Snip them from white
paper, tissue paper or tracing paper.
We used both red and white paper
for our festive display.**

Decorate simple cones of card with sequins, glitter and pompoms to create pretty tree-top angels. Feathers or leaf skeletons, which are available from art shops, make great wings. Alternatively, create a tree-top Santa Claus with red felt and a cotton-wool beard, or Rudolf the reindeer using brown card and pipe-cleaner antlers.

tree toppers

apply sequin border

Use the 30cm plate to draw out a semicircle on the card. Cut out with scissors. Glue the sequin trim around the curved edge of the semicircle, approximately 1cm from the edge. Allow to dry.

form the body Roll the card to form a cone shape. Glue the edges in place and allow to dry. You may wish to staple the join as well, to make the cone more secure.

glue on pompom head Put a dab of glue on a pompom and fix to the top of the cone. Use a silver pipe-cleaner to form a circular halo to fit on top of the pompom, and use a small amount of glue to hold it in place.

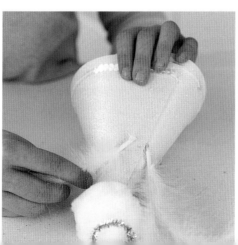

attach wings Use glue to fix the feathers at the back of the cone for the angel's wings. We used two white feathers for each wing. Allow the glue to dry completely.

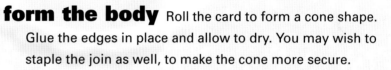

A simple cone shape in black card is the basis of this spooky witch's hat with a brim, or the simpler wizard's hat without a brim. Decorate with black net and silver stars for a night of trick or treating!

halloween hat

YOU WILL NEED:

black card • pencil • scissors • stapler or strong sticky tape • star-shaped cookie cutter to use as template • silver paper for stars • glue • black netting

measure and cut Cut out a semicircle of black card with a diameter of approximately 60cm. Roll into a cone shape and fit to the child's head. Mark out the line where the card should be joined. Use strong tape to create the cone (we used black plumber's tape, which is the same colour as the hat). A couple of staples will make the hat more secure.

cut out brim Place the cone on a sheet of black card and draw all the way around the opening. Then draw another larger circle approximately 8cm wider, to form the brim. Mark out a smaller circle 2cm within the inner circle to allow for the flaps for the brim. Cut out the brim from the card. Use scissors to cut the flaps for the brim at intervals of 2cm all the way around the inner circle.

attach hat and brim Fold alternate flaps back and sit the cone on top of the brim. Use strong sticky tape to fix the flaps to the cone. Make sure that the sticky tape is firmly pressed down to keep the brim in place.

decorate We used a star-shaped cookie cutter as a template to draw stars on silver paper. Cut them out with scissors and glue carefully to the hat. We also added a length of black netting, which we glued to the point of the hat as a finishing touch.

This fun cat mask is perfect for Halloween or a fancy-dress party. Black is the best choice for Halloween, but it would look equally cute in brown or white. Add some pipe-cleaner whiskers and a little pompom for the cat's nose.

cat mask

YOU WILL NEED:
tracing paper • black card •
black felt • glue • scissors •
pompom for nose • pipe-
cleaners for whiskers • hole
punch • length of elastic

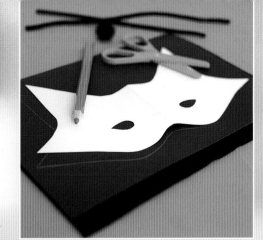

draw templates Trace the mask template on page 119 onto a piece of folded paper and cut it out. Open out the template. Take the piece of black felt and glue it to the piece of black card. Allow to dry.

cut out mask Draw around the paper template on the card side of the glued card and felt. Carefully cut out with scissors, taking particular care when cutting out the eye holes. An adult may need to help by first making a slit in the card for the eyes, so that the scissors can be easily inserted for cutting.

attach nose and whiskers Glue the pompom nose onto the mask. Cut six pipe-cleaner whiskers measuring approximately 10cm in length, and glue them to each side of the mask, just below the eye holes. Allow to dry.

attach elastic band Using a hole punch, make a hole on each side of the mask in the position indicated on the template. Thread one end of the elastic through the hole and knot to secure. Thread the elastic through the other hole, tie a knot and trim off any excess elastic to finish.

YOU WILL NEED:
white paper bag • scissors •
pencil • round paper doily •
glue • brushes for glue • pastel-
coloured cupcake cases •
stapler • hole punch • ribbon
for ties (approximately
2.5cm wide)

cut paper bag Cut off the top
edge of the paper bag, so that the
height of the bag is approximately
20cm. Draw a curve all the way from
one bottom corner of the bag to the
top, leaving the gusset edges of the
bag flat.

glue on trim Cut the curved edges of the paper doily
approximately 4cm wide. Cut another piece of doily with a
straight edge to fit the gusset edge of the bag. Glue the doily
to the inside of the hat along the curved edges and the
straight top edge, and allow to dry completely.

create rosettes Open up the cupcake cases and carefully flatten them
out. Fold each one in quarters to create a rosette shape, and attach two or three
of them to one side of the bonnet using a stapler. Fluff out the rosettes once they
are attached, so that they look like flowers.

finish off Using a hole punch,
make a hole on either side of the hat
near the bottom of the curved edge.
Thread one end of the ribbon through
one hole and knot to secure. Take the
other end of the ribbon, thread it
through the second hole, and tie a
knot to hold it in place.

easter bonnet

This cute bonnet is made from a plain paper bag decorated with the edge of a paper doily, while the delicate rosettes are made from cupcake cases. It is the perfect project for little girls to create for an Easter bonnet competition.

Real eggs painted in soft pastel colours and tied with sheer organza ribbons make a simple but effective display for Easter. Older children may like to blow the eggs first, but it is easier simply to boil them before painting and decorating.

painted eggs

YOU WILL NEED:
eggs • assorted pastel-coloured paints • selection of fine paintbrushes • egg cartons or eggcups to hold eggs for painting • sheer ribbon (approximately 1cm wide)

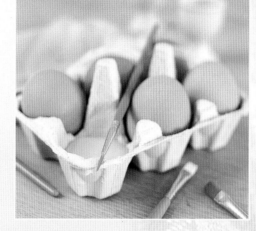

take the eggs Select the eggs and boil the required number for decorating. Allow the eggs to cool completely before you start decorating them. You may like to cut up egg cartons to hold the eggs while you are painting them.

paint eggs Paint the eggs in the chosen base colour and allow them to dry completely. You may need to apply a further coat for complete coverage. Allow to dry before adding any further decoration.

add decoration Use a fine paintbrush to add dots, swirls and stripes in a contrasting coloured paint and allow to dry thoroughly. It is easier to paint one half of the egg first, then to leave it to dry before completing the other side, to prevent the paint from smudging.

finish off Cut lengths of sheer ribbon and tie one around each egg, finishing with a bow. Group the eggs nestled together in a bowl or on a glass cakestand to create a decorative Easter display.

mother's day gift

This delicate bowl uses the traditional papier mâché technique combined with PVA glue and clingfilm, which means that the bowl can be created with fewer layers of paper for a more delicate appearance.

YOU WILL NEED:
bowl or plate to use as mould • clingfilm • newspaper • PVA glue • bowl for glue • thick brushes for glue • paint in your chosen colours • assorted brushes for painting • scissors

cover bowl Place the bowl mould upside down on a flat surface and cover with a layer of clingfilm. Tear the newspaper into strips. Paint over the clingfilm with a layer of PVA glue, then apply the first layer of paper. Repeat the process until you have built up four layers of paper. Allow to dry overnight.

lift off papier mâché bowl When it is completely dry, gently ease the papier mâché bowl away from the ceramic bowl and remove the clingfilm wrap. You can tidy the edges of the bowl with scissors, if desired.

paint the bowl Using a thick paintbrush, paint the bowl inside and out with the main colour. Allow to dry, then apply a further coat of paint. Leave to dry before applying the decoration to the bowl.

decorate We decorated the bowl with lilac and pink daisies both inside and out. You may find it easier to draw the design on the bowl in pencil first, before applying the paint. Leave to dry. A coat of water-based acrylic varnish will seal the paint and give a more hard-wearing finish.

cut simple shapes

Cut small rectangles from the wood sheet. This will be the base of the keyring. Now draw simple motifs straight onto the balsa wood and cut them out using scissors. An adult may need to assist a younger child in cutting the wood.

paint base and cutouts

Paint the base of the keyring all over the back and front and allow to dry. A further coat of paint may be necessary for even coverage. Paint the front and edges of the smaller balsa-wood pieces using a fine paintbrush. Allow to dry.

glue on motif

Apply glue to the back of the balsa-wood pieces and stick them in place on the front of the keyring. Press down firmly. Allow the glue to dry completely. You may wish to apply a coat of water-based acrylic varnish to make the keyring more hard-wearing.

attach chain

Make a small hole at the top of the keyring using a bradawl (similar to a screwdriver, with a sharp point at the end). For safety reasons, it is advisable for an adult to do this part of the project. Take the keyring attachment, thread the metal loop through the hole, and close using pliers.

These decorative keyrings are made from balsa wood and thin wood sheets, and make the perfect gift for Father's Day. Key chains are available from craft shops and are easily attached to the wood. Both boys and girls will love this easy woodwork technique.

father's day gift

valentine's day card

This three-dimensional Valentine's Day card features hearts made from decorative handmade paper. Tissue paper and paper doilies would also make pretty hearts for the card. Use pinking shears and decorative scissors (available from craft shops) to cut the paper, and finish with a ribbon bow.

YOU WILL NEED:
selection of decorative paper (scraps of wrapping paper are ideal) • blank greeting cards (or card folded in half) • pinking shears or decorative cutting scissors • glue • ribbon for bows • pencil • plain paper for template

draw hearts For the card, you need three heart shapes in decreasing sizes. Fold the decorative papers in half and press the crease flat. Draw half a heart shape in three different sizes onto three different pieces of decorative paper.

cut out hearts Use the decorative cutting scissors or pinking shears to cut around the edges of the heart motif and open it out flat. Cut out the two smaller heart shapes in the same way. If you wish, you can cut out more hearts in graduating sizes to make an even more decorative card.

layer hearts Apply a line of glue down the centre of the back of the largest heart, stick to the middle of the card and press flat. Apply glue to the centre back of the smaller heart and glue to the first heart shape on the card. Apply the smallest heart in the same way. Allow the glue to dry.

finish off Using sheer organza or velvet ribbon, cut a bow and trim the ends diagonally to prevent the ribbon fraying. Apply a small dot of glue to the central knot of the bow and stick to the heart. Leave to dry. A matching ribbon looks pretty stuck onto the back of the envelope flap, too.

YOU WILL NEED:
flowers and leaves • flower press
• glue • brushes for glue • object
for decoration (bookmark,
picture frame or greetings card) •
tweezers for lifting flowers, if
required

choose flowers It is fun to
pick flowers from the garden, but if
this is not possible use shop-bought
flowers. The flatter the flower, the
easier it is to press. If the flower is
bulky, pull off the petals, press them
individually and use them to recreate
the flower once they are pressed.

press flowers Carefully place the flowers and leaves
in the press between the layers of paper and card. Replace
the top of the flower press and tighten the screws as firmly
as you can. This ensures that as little air as possible can get
to the flowers and leaves. An adult may need to help with
tightening the screws.

remove flowers from press The flowers and leaves should be
left for about a week to make sure they are completely dry. Once they are dry,
peel them away from the papers in the press as carefully as possible, as they
become fragile once dry. Place them on a sheet of paper ready for application.

apply to desired object
Apply a thin layer of glue to the back of
a flower. Gently lift the flower and place
it in the required position (use tweezers
if necessary). Add other flowers until
the design is complete. Allow to dry
thoroughly. If decorating a box, apply
a layer of water-based acrylic varnish.

The traditional art of flower pressing will delight young children and the finished items can be used to decorate all manner of objects. We used a flower press, but leaves and flowers can be easily pressed between the pages of a heavy book or telephone directory and left for a few days to dry out.

grandma's gift

templates

pompoms
(pages 36–37)

(cut out centre)

lavender pockets
(pages 40–41)

paper flower
(pages 50–51)

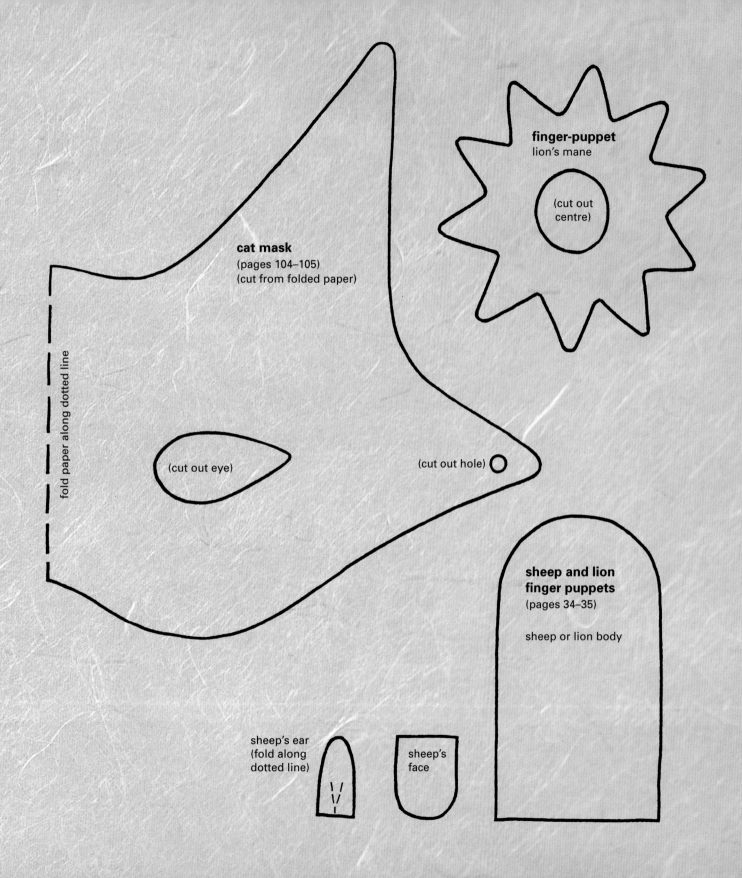

finger-puppet
lion's mane

(cut out centre)

cat mask
(pages 104–105)
(cut from folded paper)

fold paper along dotted line

(cut out eye)

(cut out hole)

sheep and lion finger puppets
(pages 34–35)

sheep or lion body

sheep's ear
(fold along
dotted line)

sheep's
face

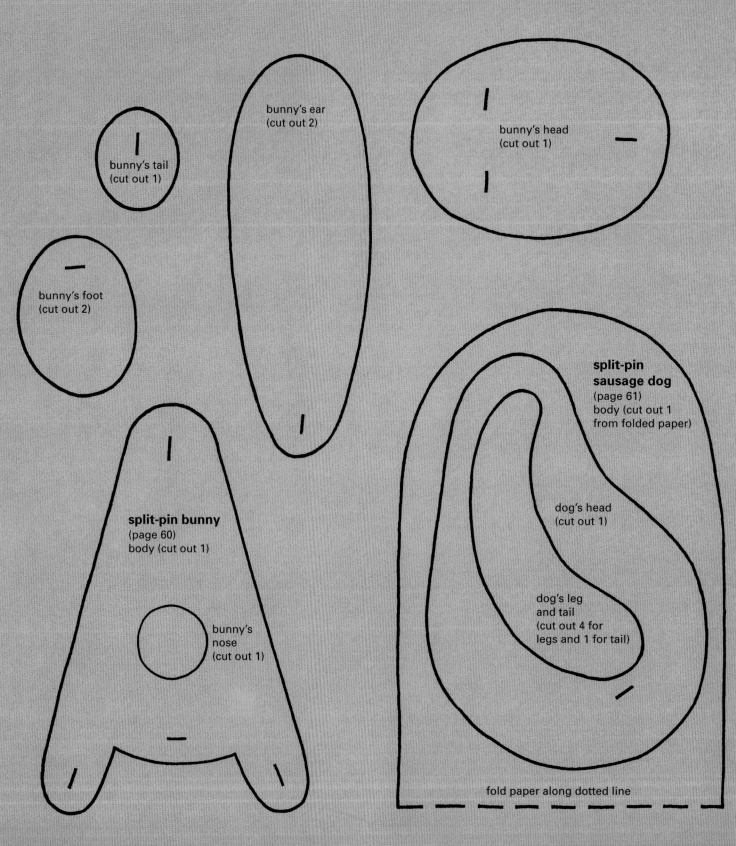

bunny's tail
(cut out 1)

bunny's ear
(cut out 2)

bunny's head
(cut out 1)

bunny's foot
(cut out 2)

split-pin bunny
(page 60)
body (cut out 1)

bunny's
nose
(cut out 1)

**split-pin
sausage dog**
(page 61)
body (cut out 1
from folded paper)

dog's head
(cut out 1)

dog's leg
and tail
(cut out 4 for
legs and 1 for tail)

fold paper along dotted line

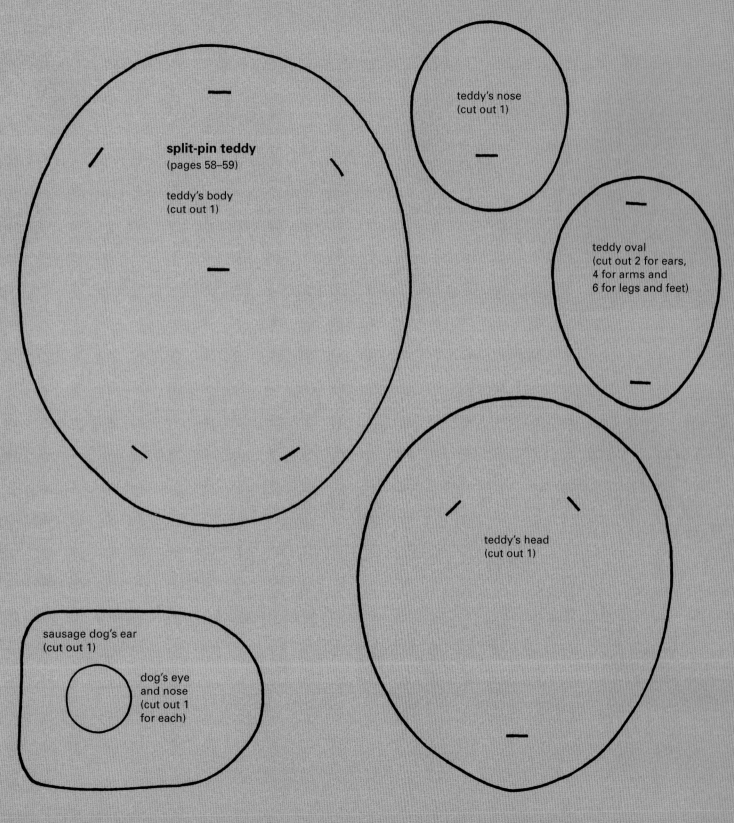

split-pin teddy
(pages 58–59)

teddy's body
(cut out 1)

teddy's nose
(cut out 1)

teddy oval
(cut out 2 for ears,
4 for arms and
6 for legs and feet)

teddy's head
(cut out 1)

sausage dog's ear
(cut out 1)

dog's eye
and nose
(cut out 1
for each)

sources

BRUSH & BISQUE-IT
85 Nightingale Lane
London SW12 8PD
020 8772 8702
www.brushandbisque-it.com
Unglazed china pieces that can be decorated with their paints and returned to the store for firing. Alternatively, decorating can be done in the shops.

CALICO CRAFTS
www.calicocrafts.co.uk
Online crafts specialist with large stock of crafting materials. Also birch ply boxes ready for decorating, as well as vintage-style labels that are ideal for découpage projects.

CATH KIDSTON
51 Marylebone High Street
London W1U 5HW
020 7935 6555
Visit www.cathkidston.co.uk for details of your nearest store.
Pretty vintage-style fabrics sold by the metre.

CONFETTI
80–81 Tottenham Court Road
London W1T 4TE
0870 774 7177
www.confetti.co.uk
Good selection of ribbons, feathers and sequins plus wrapping paper, balloons and blank cards and envelopes

CREATIONS ART AND CRAFTS MATERIALS
01326 555777
www.ecreations.co.uk
Online craft store with large stock of modelling clay, simple stitchcraft, stencils, paints, brushes, glues and more.

THE DOVER BOOKSHOP
18 Earlham Street
London WC2H 9LG
020 7836 2111
www.doverbooks.co.uk
Buy Dover books and you can photocopy their permission-, royalty- and copyright-free images and use them for découpage, or to make your own cards and wrapping paper.

EARLY LEARNING CENTRE
36 King's Road
London SW3 4HD
Call 08705 352352 or visit www.elc.co.uk for details of your nearest store.
Their craft section includes funky coloured paints, a variety of different-sized paintbrushes, felt-tip pens, plastic scissors, glue sticks, glitter pens, pompoms, coloured feathers and simple stencil designs in card and plastic – great for younger children.

ELLS & FARRIER
20 Beak Street
London W1F 9RE
020 7629 9964
www.creativebeadcraft.co.uk
The huge selection of beadas available on the website includes wood, glass, pearl and crystal designs, as well as feathers, sequins and tiny glass beads in countless colours. Also, everything you need for jewellery making, including findings such as brooch backs, clasps and other fastenings.

GREAT LITTLE TRADING CO.
Call 0870 850 6000 or visit www.gltc.co.uk for a catalogue.
Ready-mixed paint, art folders and 'paint your own...' kits.

HOBBYCRAFT
Westway Cross Shopping Park
Greenford Road
London UB6 0UW
0800 027 2387
Visit www.hobbycraft.co.uk for details of your nearest store.
Chain of craft superstores, carrying everything the young crafter needs: ribbons, feathers, pompoms, balsa wood packs, modelling clay, blank cards and envelopes, sheet card and cardboard, sequins, buttons and beads plus much more.

HOMECRAFTS DIRECT
0116 2697733
www.homecraftsdirect.co.uk
Established as a craft supplier for over ninety years, Homecrafts Direct claim to be the UK's largest arts and crafts suppliers. Log on to order hard-to-find items such as balsa wood and balsa cement, as well as craft staples such as crêpe paper, glue sticks, fabric paints, air-drying clay, ready-to-decorate face masks and instant papier-mâché mix.

IKEA
Visit www.ikea.com for a catalogue or details of your nearest store.
Good selection of wooden boxes and files and plain picture frames for decorating or découpaging. Also seasonal selections of fun decorations, wrapping paper and cards.

JANE ASHER PARTY CAKES AND SUGARCRAFT
24 Cale Street
London SW3 3QU
020 7584 6177
www.jane-asher.co.uk
Excellent selection of novelty shaped cookie cutters in both metal and plastic, plus cake frills, a variety of pretty paper doilies and coloured cake cases in many different sizes.

JOHN LEWIS

Visit www.johnlewis.co.uk for details of your nearest store.
The store's haberdashery departments are a good source for embroidery wools and cottons, felt, ribbons, buttons and sequins, as well as blank cards and dress fabrics.

KOOKS UNLIMITED

2–4 Eton Street
Richmond
Surrey TW9 1EE
020 8332 3030
www.kooksunlimited.com
Wooden spoons in assorted sizes, plus cookie cutters and jam jars with metal lids.

LAKELAND LTD

Visit www.lakelandlimited.com for details of your nearest store.
Fantastic selection of crafting products available both in the mail-order catalogue and on the website, including blank cards and envelopes, card kits, cellophane card sleeves and a huge selection of decorative

stamps and inks. Also cookie cutters, paper cake cases and bumper packs of doilies.

LETTERBOX

Call 0870 600 7878 or visit www.letterbox.co.uk for a copy of the catalogue.
Lots of fun ideas for keen crafters, such as a 'boat in a bottle' kit, or a first embroidery kit that makes a perfect gift.

MILLIE MAC

5 Sunnyside Road
Teddington
Middlesex TW11 0RP
www.milliemac.co.uk
020 8977 5779
High-quality range of hand-made children's and adults' products, ranging from oven gloves and aprons to pretty bags and bibs.

MINI MARVELLOUS

Call 0845 458 7408 or visit www.minimarvellous.co.uk for a catalogue.
Their range includes a great art desk with integral paper roll and storage space.

MOTHER GOOSE

Unit 6, Griffin Mill
London Road
Thrupp, Stroud
Gloucestershire GL5 2AZ
01453 731305
www.blanksbymothergoose.co.uk
Great selection of MDF blanks, including peg rails, trays in assorted sizes and lidded boxes, which are ideal for painting and decorating or for découpage projects.

MUJI

Visit www.muji.co.uk for details of your nearest store.
Plain boxes and notebooks, which are ideal for covering or découpage. Also pens, pencils and scissors.

PAPERCHASE

213 Tottenham Court Road
London W1T 7PS
020 7467 6200
Visit www.paperchase.co.uk for details of your nearest store.
Handmade papers, crêpe and tissue paper and card. Also blank cards and envelopes in many colours and sizes.

SELWYN-SMITH STUDIOS

148 High Street
Teddington
Middlesex TW11 8HZ
020 8973 0771
Paper, pens, pencils, brushes and paint dishes.

SEWING & CRAFT SUPERSTORE

296–312 Balham High Road
London SW17 7AA
020 8767 0036

www.craftysewer.com
Everything from beads and sequins to blank cards, felt, pompoms, wool, buttons and pipe-cleaners.

THE STENCIL LIBRARY

Stocksfield Hall
Northumberland
NE43 7TN
01661 844 844
www.stencil-library.com
Decorative stencils, from simple shapes to complicated all-over designs, plus water-based stencil paints and brushes. Paints can be used on walls, furniture and fabric.

URCHIN

Call 0870 112 6006 or visit www.urchin.co.uk for a catalogue.
Bumper craft packs as well as craft kits that make great gifts.

VV ROULEAUX

6 Marylebone High Street
London W1M 3PB
020 7224 5179
Visit www.vvrouleaux.com for details of their other stores.
A vast selection of ribbons from taffeta and velvet to embroidered cotton plus beaded motifs, pompoms, pretty trims, feather birds and fabric flowers.

WOOLWORTHS

Visit www.woolworths for details of your nearest store.
Basic range of craft materials including paper, paints, felt-tips, glitter glue and assorted collage materials.

picture credits

ALL PHOTOGRAPHY BY VANESSA DAVIES

PAINT: pages 8–9 paints from Hobbycraft, paint dishes from Selwyn-Smith Studios, brushes from Sewing & Craft Superstore, Early Learning Centre; **pages 10–11** paints and plate from Brush & Bisque-It, striped aprons by Millie Mac; **pages 12–13** picture frame from Cargo Homeshop, plate from Brush & Bisque-It, tray from Mother Goose; **pages 14–15** potato printing paints from Hobbycraft, cookie cutter from Jane Asher Party Cakes; **pages 16–17** paper from Paperchase, calico fabric from John Lewis, picture frames and ribbon from IKEA; **pages 18–19** paints from Hobbycraft; **pages 20–21** paints from Hobbycraft; **pages 22–23** paints from Hobbycraft, fabric-covered notebooks from Paperchase; **pages 24–25** wooden lidded box from IKEA , heart and soldier stencils, brush and stencil paint from The Stencil Library; **pages 26–27** calico and bias binding for aprons from John Lewis, stencils from The Stencil Library

FABRIC: pages 28–29 materials, satin ribbons and wool from John Lewis, velvet ribbons and pipe cleaners from Paperchase, felt and pins from Sewing & Craft Superstore; **page 30–31** ribbons from Paperchase and John Lewis; **pages 32–33** projects coloured pipe-cleaners from Paperchase, ribbons from John Lewis and Paperchase; **pages 34–35** felt and three-dimensional fabric pens from Sewing & Craft Superstore; **pages 36–37** pompoms wool from John Lewis; **pages 38–39** wool from John Lewis, wool fabric from Sewing & Craft Superstore; **pages 40–41** lavender pockets felt, ribbon and buttons from Sewing & Craft Superstore; **pages 42–43** collage felt, fabrics and glue from Sewing & Craft Superstore, lolly sticks from Hobbycraft; **pages 44–45** floral fabrics and spot china from Cath Kidston, tray (unpainted MDF) by Mother Goose, plain fabrics from Sewing & Craft Superstore, spot ribbon and trim on teacosy from VV Rouleaux; **pages 46–47** dyes from Sewing & Craft Superstore

PAPER: pages 48–49 crêpe paper, pipe-cleaners and card all from Paperchase; **pages 50–53** crêpe paper, blank cards and card all from Paperchase; **pages 54–55** paper from Paperchase, tassels from John Lewis, glitter and glue from Sewing & Craft Superstore, orange scissors from Early Learning Centre; **pages 56–57** coloured paper from Sewing & Craft Superstore, wood from Hobbycraft; **pages 58–61** card from Sewing & Craft Superstore; **pages 62–63** paper from Paperchase; **pages 64–65** handmade papers and notebooks from Paperchase; **pages 66–67** projects boxes from Hobbycraft, handmade papers from Paperchase; **pages 68–69** paper from Paperchase, ribbon from Sewing & Craft Superstore; **pages 70–71** découpage handmade papers from Sewing & Craft Superstore, box from Muji; **pages 72–73** black-and-white playing-card paper from Dover Books, handmade papers from Paperchase, floral wallpaper from Laura Ashley, velvet ribbon from Sewing & Craft Superstore

MODELLING: pages 74–75 cookie cutters from Jane Asher Party Cakes, wooden spoons from Kooks Unlimited, wire from Hobbycraft; **pages 78–81** balsa wood, paints, lolly sticks and peg doll from Hobbycraft, gingham from Sewing & Craft Superstore; **pages 82–83** jam jars from Kooks Unlimited, glitter from Hobbycraft, decorations from Homebase; **pages 84–85** clay and paints from Hobbycraft, cookie cutters from Jane Asher Party Cakes and Kooks Unlimited, paint dish from Selwyn-Smith

Studios; **pages 86–87** cookie cutters from Kooks Unlimited, butterfly, flower and fish cookie cutters from Jane Asher Party Cakes, ribbon from VV Rouleaux, magnets and brooch backs from Sewing & Craft Superstore; **pages 88–89** wooden spoons from Kooks Unlimited, floral fabric from Cath Kidston, felt from Sewing & Craft Superstore, paper doilies from Jane Asher Party Cakes; **pages 90–91** wooden beads and wire from Sewing & Craft Superstore, plain coloured beads and wire from Hobbycraft, glasses with beads from IKEA; **pages 92–93** balsa wood, paint, beads, modelling clay and wire all from Hobbycraft

SPECIAL OCCASIONS: pages 94–95 peg dolls, sequins and glitter from Hobbycraft, pompom, glitter and sheer ribbon from Sewing & Craft Superstore, paint plate from Selwyn-Smith Studios, cupcake cases and doilies from Jane Asher Party Cakes; **pages 96–97** peg dolls from Hobbycraft, ribbon, lace and silver card from Sewing & Craft Superstore; **pages 98–99** red and white paper from Hobbycraft; **pages 100–101** glitter card from Paperchase, sequins, pompoms and silver pipe-cleaner from Sewing & Craft Superstore, Christmas tree and lights from Woolworths; **pages 102–103** black card, silver paper and black netting from Sewing & Craft Superstore, scissors from Early Learning Centre; **pages 104–105** black card, black felt, pompom, elastic and pipe-cleaners from Sewing & Craft Superstore, pencil and scissors from Early Learning Centre; **pages 106–107** doilies and cupcases from Jane Asher Party Cakes, sheer ribbon from Confetti; **pages 108–109** sheer ribbons and paintbrushes from Sewing & Craft Superstore, paints from Hobbycraft; **pages 110–111** paints and brushes from Hobbycraft; **pages 112–113** balsa and strip wood and paints from Hobbycraft, brushes and keyring chains from Sewing & Craft Superstore; **pages 114–115** cards and paper from Paperchase, ribbons and decorative paper from Sewing & Craft Superstore; **pages 116–117** wooden picture frames from IKEA, handmade papers from Paperchase

index

acknowledgments Thank you to Vanessa Davies for her beautiful photography and attention to detail in the wonderful pictures she shot for the book. Thanks to Catherine Griffin and Annabel Morgan for their help in all stages of the book – its design, layout and words. Thank you to all the fantastic children who modelled for the book – their patience during photography and their enthusiasm for the projects they worked on. Thanks also to Hobbycraft for supplying wooden beads and The Stencil Library for the stencils. Finally, a big thank you to my husband Michael for his unfailing support and the delicious suppers he made when I had to work late to finish the projects for the book.